SO-BFA-265

Blue Window

A COMEDY

by Craig Lucas

SAMUEL FRENCH, INC.

45 WEST 25TH STREET   NEW YORK 10010

7623 SUNSET BOULEVARD   HOLLYWOOD 90046

LONDON   *TORONTO*

Copyright © 1984, 1985 by Craig Lucas

ALL RIGHTS RESERVED

CAUTION: Professionals and amateurs are hereby warned that BLUE WINDOW is subject to a royalty. It is fully protected under the copyright laws of the United States of America, the British Commonwealth, including Canada, and all other countries of the Copyright Union. All rights, including professional, amateur, motion pictures, recitation, lecturing, public reading, radio broadcasting, television, and the rights of translation into foreign languages are strictly reserved. In its present form the play is dedicated to the reading public only.

The amateur live stage performance rights to BLUE WINDOW are controlled exclusively by Samuel French, Inc., and royalty arrangements and licenses must be secured well in advance of presentation. PLEASE NOTE that amateur royalty fees are set upon application in accordance with your producing circumstances. When applying for a royalty quotation and license please give us the number of performances intended, dates of production, your seating capacity and admission fee. Royalties are payable one week before the opening performance of the play to Samuel French, Inc., at 45 W. 25th Street, New York, NY 10010; or at 7623 Sunset Blvd., Hollywood, CA 90046, or to Samuel French (Canada), Ltd., 80 Richmond Street East, Toronto, Ontario, Canada M5C 1P1.

Royalty of the required amount must be paid whether the play is presented for charity or gain and whether or not admission is charged.

Stock royalty quoted on application to Samuel French, Inc.

For all other rights than those stipulated above, apply to Peter Franklin, William Morris Agency, Inc. 1350 Avenue of the Americas, New York, NY 10019.

Particular emphasis is laid on the question of amateur or professional readings, permission and terms for which must be secured in writing from Samuel French, Inc.

Copying from this book in whole or in part is strictly forbidden by law, and the right of performance is not transferable.

Whenever the play is produced the following notice must appear on all programs, printing and advertising for the play: "Produced by special arrangement with Samuel French, Inc."

Due authorship credit must be given on all programs, printing and advertising for the play.

ISBN 0 573 61954 9   Printed in U.S.A.

No one shall commit or authorize any act or omission by which the copyright of, or the right to copyright, this play may be impaired.

No one shall make any changes in this play for the purpose of production.

Publication of this play does not imply availability for performance. Both amateurs and professionals considering a production are *strongly* advised in their own interests to apply to Samuel French, Inc., for written permission before starting rehearsals, advertising, or booking a theatre.

No part of this book may be reproduced, stored in a retrieval system, or transmitted in any form, by any means, now known or yet to be invented, including mechanical, electronic, photocopying, recording, videotaping, or otherwise, without the prior written permission of the publisher.

IMPORTANT BILLING AND CREDIT REQUIREMENTS

All producers of BLUE WINDOW *must* give credit to the Author of the Play in all programs distributed in instances in which the title of the Play appears for purposes of advertising, publicizing or otherwise exploiting the Play and/or a production. The name of the Author *must* also appear on a separate line, on which no other name appears, immediately following the title, and *must* appear in size of type not less than fifty percent the size of the title type.

Sheet music for "The Same Thing (Office Girl's) Lament", words and music by William Bolcom is available for $2.50, plus postage. This song is to be used in productions of BLUE WINDOW. In all programs used in connection with productions of the Plays, William Bolcom must be credited as the Author of both words and music to this song.

BLUE WINDOW was originally produced by The Production Company, Norman Rene, Artistic Director, Abigail Franklin, Managing Director at Theater Guinevere with the following cast:

EMILY	Maureen Silliman
TOM	Lawrence Joshua
LIBBY	Randy Danson
NORBERT	Matt Craven
BOO	Christine Estabrook
GRIEVER	Brad O'Hare
ALICE	Margo Skinner

The production was directed by Norman Rene; Setting by Loy Arcenas; Lighting by Debra J. Kletter; Costumes by Walker Hicklin, Production Stage Manager, M.A. Howard. The first performance was on May 28, 1984.

CHARACTERS
(in order of appearance)

EMILY
TOM
LIBBY
NORBERT
BOO
GRIEVER
ALICE

SCENE ONE occurs in five separate New York apartments simultaneously. SCENE TWO is in Libby's apartment, shortly after Scene One. SCENE THREE returns to four of the original five apartments later that same evening; again they are seen simultaneously.

THE TIME is Sunday evening, 1984.

(NOTE: *Blue Window* was written as a developmental project for the Production Company. Its shape grew out of discussions with director Norman Rene, designers, actors and crew. All stage directions herein reflect their contributions. I have included these stage directions as a kind of a blueprint—a map to the original production and its intent. They are there if you need them and to be ignored if not.

Simultaneous dialogue appears in separate columns with the main theme generally to the left and counterpoint or accompaniment to the right. The softer the actors speak during simultaneous passages the easier it is to hear the words. When two lines begin on the same line the actors begin at the same time and then proceed at their own pace.)

5

for Dr. Tim

Blue Window

(*In the darkness*)

VOICE. Uno, due, tre, quattro, cinque, sei, sette . . .

(*Lights up slowly. Birds; traffic. EMILY stands alone. She is dressed for a cool day. The floor, walls and upstage scrim are all a light blue. Five open doorways stage left. Black, sculptural shapes flecked with bright confetti markings represent furniture: down right is LIBBY's bar unit. Up right, ALICE and BOO's sofa unit. Center, TOM and EMILY's ottoman. Up left, NORBERT's armchair. Down left, GRIEVER's dressing unit and mirror. Up stage, slightly tilted towards the audience, hangs a large, transparent canvas, framed like a window, splattered with bright paint. Several smaller units hold flowers and phones. The feeling is open and attractive; only a little sterile.*)

EMILY unwraps and chews a piece of gum. TOM enters with sheet music, pencil, beer. We hear the song he is trying to write, in fits and starts. He makes a correction in the music and we hear the altered melody. EMILY crosses upstage behind the canvas, visible through the splashes of paint. LIBBY enters in her raincoat, glasses, rainbonnet, black scarf. She has a bag of groceries, her handbag, her keys in her mouth and cigarette in hand. The keys go into the handbag, the cigarette into her mouth, the groceries set down, coat off revealing a slip underneath. She exits on classical music which brings on NORBERT in exercise outfit, carrying an orange and a record jacket.

LIBBY re-enters with two lists—TO DO and TO BUY—which she tacks up on the wall. NORBERT begins to assemble a jigsaw puzzle, seated on the back on his chair, puzzle in lap. Typing from offstage. LIBBY exits. BOO enters with a small, dying plant which she places by the big canvas. She talks to the plant in hushed tones of affection. Bored, she sits and listens to a language tape, quickly losing interest. LIBBY re-enters with a kitchen timer which she is winding; she now wears a loose, flowing kimono. BOO changes the tape on her Walkman. LIBBY goes off and comes back, looking for her handbag which is under her arm. BOO jogs to the music which we do not hear. Discouraged at the size of her thighs, she tosses off headphones and exits as GRIEVER, in his bathrobe, enters: dance music. Checks himself in mirror, lays out new clothes. BOO re-enters with cigarette and ashtray. LIBBY has gone and come again, this time with a bowl of mussels and knife, trying hopelessly to open the shells. GREIVER has gone off and returned with shoes. The music gets to him and he dances around the stage into each of the other character's territories, finally exiting to take his shower; music fades. TOM picks up guitar, plays first part of his song. Typing from off. Typing stops. By now LIBBY has cut her finger and gone off for a band-aid. BOO, unable to find a single matchbook with a match in it, has tossed her last cigarette across the room; she finds a match, lights cigarette and walks several times around her sofa as if she might get somewhere, eventually. NORBERT has peeled his orange, eaten it, and is still assembling his puzzle. EMILY has crossed further left behind the painting.)

TOM. (*to someone unseen, offstage*) Do you like this? It should like . . . I like the fact that it doesn't go anywhere. I mean, I can hear the whole thing. Like I did this and I did this and then this happened and this happened and so what? It should be kind of bland, you know, and flat out . . . (*LIBBY comes on with seven place-cards.*) Do you know anybody who writes lyrics? I mean, I don't even think I would want it to rhyme. And the voice should have the melody without any beefing up, it should be thin, and the guitar stays constant. Like just one awful thing after another. I can hear it . . . I just can't . . .

LIBBY. (*going through place-cards, unable to assign the last card a name*) Alice, Boo, Emily, Tom . . . Norbert. Alice, Boo, Emily, Tom, Norbert . . . Griever.

TOM. Like I went here and I did this and I did this and I went here and I did this and I did this . . .

LIBBY. (*continued*) Alice, Boo, Emily . . . Tom . . . Alice, Boo, Emily . . . LIBBY! Libby, Libby, Libby, Libby . . .

TOM. (*continued*) Maybe it'd sound better on a piano. God, I used to have this beautiful, beautiful piano, real nice touch, baby grand . . . You know who got it. "The kids'll want to take piano lessons . . . Get your own piano." Duh, it is my own piano. Nobody's going to take piano lessons, I can guarantee . . . (*LIBBY exits.*) I just don't want this to sound like a folk song . . .

ALICE. (*entering, high from her work*) "Moonlight and love songs never out of date/Hearts full of passion, jealousy and hate—" (*Kisses BOO on top of her head; BOO is again listening to her language tape.*) What are we listening to? "Woman needs man!"

BOO. What?

ALICE. Eye-talian?

Boo. Si.

ALICE. Are we bringing wine or flowers or what?

Boo. (*overlapping the last few words*) Never on Sunday, remember? It's Sunday.

ALICE. We didn't drink the whole case, did we? What do you mean "we," white man? (*LIBBY re-enters with cookbook, phone and hammer; she dials.*)

Boo. Breakthrough? (*GRIEVER's phone rings.*)

ALICE. I don't know, maybe. Maybe not. (*BOO puts her headphones back on.*) I can take the hint, never mind.

Boo. What?

ALICE. (*exiting*) Niente. Impari il tuo Italiano.

GRIEVER. (*rushes on, dripping wet, with towel, answers the phone*) I'm coming. I've got my coat on.

LIBBY. Did you ever do mussels?

GRIEVER. I'm not sure I know what you mean.

LIBBY. Never mind, Griever, never mind, here it is, they steam themselves open, goodbye. (*She hangs up.*)

GRIEVER. Goodbye to you. (*into mirror*) And you and you. And alllllllll the little people. The little tiny Irish people. (*LIBBY exits.*) Goodbye, goodbyyyyyyeee. Auf wiedersehen. Goodnight. We hate to say goodbye. We hate to see you leave, but get out. Go home, go home— A dog with his bone. I am so embarrassed for you. (*puts on pants*) I am so embarrassed for your family. I am so embarrassed for the children and their queen. Debbie. (*belt*)

ALICE. (*back on*) Kiss me.

GRIEVER. Queen Debbie.

Boo. What?

GRIEVER. Debbie the queen of the debutantes.

ALICE. Kiss me.

Boo. I can't, my mother is at the airport. "La mia mama e all'aeroporto."

ALICE. Really. Uh-huh. (*taking both sides of an imaginary conversation*) "Marry me." "I can't, my umbrella is in the kitchen." "Then run away with me."

Boo. What?

ALICE. "I can't, the highway is pink."
"Then shoot me for godsake." "I can't, this is a dessert cheese."

Boo. What are we talking about?

ALICE. (*exiting*)
You could just say my breath smells, it's fine.

GRIEVER. (*quietly*)
And her husband Norbert. (*begins putting on socks and shoes*)

GRIEVER. Norbert is embarrassed for all the little people . . . The little people are ashamed . . . And Stan Hopewell, the maker of so many pretty little shoes is proud to be ashamed of queen Debbie who by a strange coincidence of marriage and surgery is in fact her own uncle—by marriage to what should have been her second cousin once removed but is now as I say by a fluke of bloodsmanship a small but elegant . . . electric peanut. (*picks up brush to polish shoes, treats it as an Academy award*) Thank you. Thank you. This means so much to me. I

ALICE. (*back on, munching a cracker*) I'm going to get flowers.

would never have been able to play this part if not for the unerring dedication, the unquestioned brilliance and the small shoes of . . . Yo mothuh! That's right I said yo muthuh! Yo!

Boo. Why are you eating? Where are you going?

GRIEVER. (*overlapping the last few words*) Yo, Stella!

ALICE. (*from off*) I'M GOING TO GET FLOWERS, GRANDMOTHER! (*pops head in door*) Relax, mia amore, bambina! (*blows kisses and exits*)

GRIEVER. STELLLL-AAAAAAA! (*exits, re-enters on Motown music with hair drier*)

GRIEVER. Thank you. Thank you thank you thank you. And now go home. Go home and drive safely. (*blows hair drier in face like a heavy storm*) Leave the park now. It's raining too hard. I know, I know, but the safest thing is for us all to leave, so I want you to move slowly and safely, directly out of the park. Be careful of your neighbor. I want you to turn to the man next to you and I want you to slit his throat. I want you to spill his blood, motherfucker . . . (*Hair drier off; it becomes a microphone.*) Thank you. There isn't anything I can say. (*LIBBY has returned with a drink; reading the back of the rum bottle, she has discovered a recipe and dials the phone.*) I love you. I do. You're my main . . . main . . . mlaaaaaa. Mlaaaa-mlaaaaaa. We're tired now, goodnight. (*He exits; phone rings.*)

TOM. Which sounds better? (*Plays guitar. GRIEVER returns, answers phone.*)

GRIEVER. I am out the door.

LIBBY. Just tell me if
this sounds tacky. One
part rum— One part un-
diluted pineapple juice
concentrate   GRIEVER. It sounds
from a can, listen, one   tacky. Tacky, tacky . . .
part triple sec, grenadine,
lemon
or   TOM. Or.
lime slices and confec-
tionary sugar to taste.

GRIEVER. Where does it say about the glucose tolerance test we're all going to have to take when we get to the hospital—?

LIBBY. (*hanging up before he has finished his sentence*) Goodbye.

GRIEVER. Goodbye. Goodbye.

TOM. None of the above?

LIBBY. (*making the punch*) I really love your books, Alice. No. You know what I love, Alice? May I? Call you? By the way I am absolutely crazy about your books, oh sure, hasn't everybody? Bleah. Oh, are you a writer? I didn't realize that. Alice Fisher, my god. Everyone, this is Alice Fisher and her lover, Boo Boo.

GRIEVER. (*trying on shirts*) No.

LIBBY. So how's the new book coming, Alice? What? Are you serious? You can't stop writing. You're one of the best writers of our generation—

GRIEVER. (*holding up another shirt*) No.

LIBBY. My generation—

GRIEVER. No.

LIBBY. Your genera-
tion. How old are you,

Alice? Seriously, would you mind inscribing my copy of GLISSANDO? Oh sure, I've only read it about ten times. My favorite character? Well, I'd have to say I liked them all equally . . . There's only one? Character. Well, it's just she's like so many different people I know . . . He. Is. Soooooo you (*dialing*) girls are lesbians.

GRIEVER. (*shirt after shirt*) Charming, but— No. . . . Well, how you say—No. Thank you . . . No. Very nice and . . . No. No thank you. No no no. . . . No . . . Nnnnnn-nnnnmaybe.

No.

TOM. This is the bridge.

(*Phone rings; GRIEVER answers.*)

GRIEVER. I've left, I'm on my way.

LIBBY. (*not waiting for him to finish his lines*) Stop on your way and pick up a copy of Alice Fisher's new book would you please for me?

GRIEVER. I want you to listen to the sound of my voice.

LIBBY. I can't.

GRIEVER. Take a deeeep breath.

LIBBY. I can't, I can't—

GRIEVER. Iiiiiiinnnnnnn—

LIBBY. I'm having a break-down. (*hangs up*) I love your books, I just read the new one, I mean, I just bought the new one, but—I lent it, what a great title, I loved it, I love your new book, what's it called? What I love, Alice, what I really really love about your books are the covers, I always judge a book by its cover, don't you? No, seriously, I love the way you weave all the different strands together, all the different people in different places doing different things, it's like modern music. How is it like modern music? . . . I don't know. (*BOO exits. LIBBY has dialed.*)

TOM. See, it takes like a long time to resolve and then it just goes to the same refrain over and over, you know, like a Chinese screen. It's like one stroke and that's the whole thing. I wish I I had . . . I can hear it . . .

GRIEVER. (*another shirt*) YES! Yes, yes, yes! . . . . No . . . . Yes . . . . No . . . . Nnnnnnnnnnnn-nnnnyes . . .

No . . . . Maybe . . . . Maybe . . . . Maybe . . . Nnnnnnooo . . . . Maybe . . .

GRIEVER. (*answering*) I am in the taxi—

LIBBY. It's off.

GRIEVER. I am there, I'm ringing your bell—

LIBBY. No, I'm not going to be here, I'm going to the movies—

GRIEVER. Listen to me please—

LIBBY. I died.

GRIEVER. It is the guest's responsibility to have a good time. You provide the space—

LIBBY. I got sick and died.

GRIEVER. Then it is up to the guest. If he or she does not choose to have a good time—

LIBBY. They won't.

TOM. (continued; singing and playing) "I came here to—

I came down to . . ."

Something . . . "I came

here from—" . . .

"They all want the same

thing . . ."

TOM. (continued) What's the story?

TOM. Are we going?

GRIEVER. There is nothing you can do about it.

TOM. Are we going?

GRIEVER. Conversely, no amount of burnt food, bad wine, cheap cocaine or hideous furnishings—

TOM. Em?

GRIEVER. (not stopping) Can prevent the truly convivial spirit from having a pleasant evening in the company of his or her peers.

LIBBY. Thank you.

GRIEVER. Now go vomit. I will be right—(She hangs up.) There, goodbye—

TOM. Baby?

GRIEVER. Goodbye, goodbye—(the right shirt) Yes!

LIBBY. No, I love your books, I really do. I said I love your books, Alice, don't you know how to take a compliment? That's not a very attractive trait, Alice. Maybe that's something you'd like to think about, work on with your friend, your lesbian, lover, doctor friend, I'll tell you something, Alice (*ALICE enters.*) You lay down with psychiatrists, you get up with flaws.

GRIEVER. . . . . . . Yes, yes, yes!

ALICE. It's warm.

LIBBY. (*on her exit*) No, I love your books, really, Catcher in the Raw, for instance.

BOO. (*from off*) Time to go?

ALICE. If only I hadn't run into her in the elevator that day. (*BOO enters, drying her hair with a towel.*) I was just so pleased I remembered her name. I hate that name, it sounds like something you put on Indian food: Libby. Please pass the Libby.

BOO. Are we going as we are or, uh—?

ALICE. It's all my fault. Why don't I call and say I'm sick, I don't mind . . . You hate me.

(*BOO exits as EMILY enters from outside.*)

TOM. What was that all about?

EMILY. You were working.

TOM. I'm having a conversation with myself like an asshole.

EMILY. Oh. I'm sorry.

TOM. . . . Nice out?

EMILY. Yeah. How'd it go?

TOM. Good. Needs words.

EMILY. Can I hear?

TOM. Well, are we going?

EMILY. Oh—I'll just fix my hair. (*She exits as BOO comes on, wearing a different blouse.*) Who are these people, remind me.

LIBBY. (*re-enters in black cocktail dress*) Alice, Boo, Emily, Tom . . .

TOM. Nobody. Listen, this part is pretty.

ALICE. We can stay in . . . How 'bout if we have a signal for when one of us wants to leave?

LIBBY. (*introduces the place-cards to one another*) Alice, this is Tom. Tom, this is Alice. Alice, Emily, Booby, Boober . . . Boo Boo . . . Bee Boo Boo . . . Booby Boo Boo . . . Bebe Rebozo . . . . . . Bobby Goldsboro . . . (*throws place-cards away*)

BOO. I'll just scream.

ALICE. Or I could say something like . . .

ALICE. Or I could say

BOO. Time to go now.

ALICE. That's good. (*BOO goes off.*)

TOM. Do you want to hear this?

GRIEVER. (*trying on the first tie*) Nope.

EMILY. (*from off*) I'm listening. (*enters*) Sorry.

ALICE. (*calling to offstage*) You look terrific!

GRIEVER. No way.

TOM. Okay. It has like a melody—sort of a descant over the top. (*BOO re-enters, tying sash around her waist.*)

EMILY. Uh-huh.

ALICE. I, on the other hand, look like an old, used . . .

TOM. And the whole thing should be on a piano, but we don't have a piano, so . . . (*NORBERT exits.*)

BOO. True. Let's go.

TOM. All right?

ALICE. It's right downstairs.

TOM. It needs words.

BOO. Then let's be early.

EMILY. Okay.

BOO. Nouvelle chic. (*LIBBY goes out again; TOM plays.*)

ALICE. You just want to see her with her hair wet.

BOO. Absolutely.

ALICE. (*looking in compact mirror*) Wait. God.

BOO. You look fine.

ALICE. I don't want anybody to think I labored to look this . . .

EMILY. Pretty.

ALICE. Unlabored.

EMILY. I like it.

ALICE. It's true:

TOM. Wait, this is the melody.

GRIEVER. Tooooooooo.

TOM. I mean, it's not in the accompaniment . . . Well, you'll see . . . . I know what it should say, too, but . . . Like this . . .

ALICE. You have to put yourself together a little bit or people think you think you're so cool you don't have to put yourself together.

BOO. (*exiting yet again*) Vanity, vanity, all is . . .

TOM. Without words. (*plays*)

ALICE. I'm so vain I prob'ly think this song is about me. (*LIBBY re-enters with hor d'oeuvres; she tries to get top off caviar jar.*)

Tom. Or something. It keeps repeating.

Boo. (*from off*) Fairfield Porter?

Alice. The—? Famous?

Boo. (*entering*) Painter?

Alice. Right.

Boo. When asked if he thought it was vain to sign one's paintings or not to sign one's paintings . . .

Alice. Right.

Boo. Said—

Alice. To sign or not to sign.

Boo. Right.

Tom. This is the bridge.

Alice. Said?

Boo. If you're vain, then it's vain to sign your paintings and it's vain not to sign your paintings.

Alice. Ah-ha. (*LIBBY bangs caviar jar twice on table top.*)

Boo. And if you're not vain, then it's not vain to sign your paintings and it's not vain—

Alice and Boo. Not to sign your paintings.

Alice. Too true. And we would say that I am—?

Emily. It's like a folk song. (*LIBBY breaks her cap, trying to pry open the caviar jar.*)

Libby. Ow! (*TOM stops playing.*)

Emily. It's not like a folk song. (*LIBBY spits out her tooth.*)

Alice. No comment.	Tom.
All right, let's go.	Let's go.

Emily. It isn't.

Tom. It is, come on.

(*ALICE is headed for the door; NORBERT returns in different clothes, picks up puzzle, orange peel and exits.*)

Boo. Flowers.

Emily. It's pretty.

Tom. Yeah.

Emily. I like it.

Alice. This is why I keep you around.

Tom. It's supposed to be the way it is, exactly the way it is.

Alice.	Emily.
All right, what's our signal?	I know.
Boo.	Tom.
You say, Did anybody see that article in the Times on DNA? And I'll say—	The words are
Alice. No, I didn't see that—	completely un-sentimental—
Boo. Wasn't it incredible?	Emily. Uh-huh.

Alice.	Tom.	Griever. (answers)
Oh, okay, wasn't it—	They're flat, like I did this and I did this and I—	Walk directly to your front door and by the time
Boo. No, if I want to leave I'll say yes and if I don't I'll say no.		
Alice. Good.		you get there I will be there. (hangs up)

(LIBBY has dialed; phone rings.)

LIBBY. Grieve?
EMILY. I like it.
ALICE. Wait.
BOO. What?
ALICE. I love you.
TOM. I like you.
GRIEVER. Yes!

(*Black out. Lights up to half. The actors move the black, sculptural pieces into their positions for the party. TOM's ottoman becomes the coffee table. GRIEVER's dressing table becomes a chair, etc. In the half-light we see ALICE present LIBBY with the flowers; she then places them in a vase. All of this is underscored with melancholy piano music. As the party lights come up all the actors are frozen in position: BOO and GRIEVER at the punch bowel, NORBERT down left, TOM and EMILY on the sofa, ALICE upstage center and LIBBY standing. Large pillows have been placed on the floor around the coffee table.*)

SCENE 2

ALICE. (*As she speaks the other characters are released from their freeze.*) There's this whole theory, all right?
BOO. (*GRIEVER fills her punch glass.*) Here we go.
ALICE. That the experiential part of the brain — The right? Hemisphere?
BOO. (*overlapping*) Don't look at me.
ALICE. And the side responsible for assigning the words . . .

GRIEVER. Right.

ALICE. No, the left. Ha ha. Are incompatible.

GRIEVER. Alice.

ALICE. Essentially. Essentially.

BOO. Wellllll—

ALICE. They don't communicate.

BOO. If they didn't communicate—

ALICE. They barely communicate, I'm telling this, if you want to make up your own theory—

BOO. That's right—

ALICE. When I'm finished making up mine . . .

GRIEVER. The experiential part and the part—

ALICE. Right. And there's just this little thread connecting the two. Called—the corpus cassolum.

GRIEVER. I knew that.

ALICE. Right?

BOO. Callosum.

ALICE. Callosum, the corpus callosum. And that's all there is. (*LIBBY exits into kitchen.*) So everything that happens in the right side of the brain and everything that happens in the left side of the brain has to pass through this little thread. If the right hand is to know what the left hand is doing so to speak.

GRIEVER. Write that down.

ALICE. Anyway. You're trying to capture the intangible.

GRIEVER. Uh-huh? (*LIBBY re-enters with a tray of canapes which she takes from guest to guest.*)

ALICE. And you can't. Because the experience doesn't want to be captured. The way primitive peoples don't want to have their pictures taken.

BOO. Why are you looking at me?

ALICE. So you're constantly jumping back and forth: "What did that feel like?" "What do you call that?" And the words are always less. Or maybe I'm just a mediocre writer.

Boo. Right.

ALICE.   LIBBY. (*serving ALICE*)
So the thing that—   Oh, I really love—

ALICE. (*continued*) I'm sorry.

LIBBY. (*holding her top lip in place with one finger*) I say I really love your writing.

ALICE. Oh, thank you. Thank you. No, it's, you know, that feeling of its being right on the tip of your tongue.

GRIEVER. Right.   TOM. Uh-huh.

ALICE. And nine hundred and ninety nine times out of a thousand: Smoke, nothing, blah.

GRIEVER. I hate that. Don't you? When you can't . . . when you can't . . . think of something (*laugh, to LIBBY*) Smile. (*She does, without showing teeth.*) That's better.

ALICE. So you can't wait for inspiration is my point.

GRIEVER. Uh-huh.

ALICE. That's all. You have to work.

GRIEVER. Right.

ALICE. Which is why I'm such a bore to live with. (*LIBBY is serving BOO.*)

Boo. Here, here, I'll drink to that.

GRIEVER. But . . .

Boo. This punch is so tacky, I love it.

LIBBY. (*towards the wall*) Thanks.

GRIEVER. All right. How do you know. . . ? You'll have to forgive me, I'm illiterate. But . . . I mean, how do you know—? Or—I mean . . . Come on, Griever, you can do it.

ALICE. See, you could never name a character Griever, for instance, without everybody wanting to know

'What's he grieving?'

GRIEVER. Right.

ALICE. For. Is it grieving for or grieving?

Boo. Grieving for.   LIBBY. Grieving.

ALICE. Is it?

TOM. Grieving for, I think.

ALICE. I never learned any grammar either, so — Anyway, how do you know what?

GRIEVER. Well, how do you know—? I mean, do you know everything that's going to happen in a certain story?

ALICE. No.

GRIEVER. Before you start?

ALICE. I don't. You just — jump off the cliff. You're bound to land somewhere. And you never know — I mean — if I might borrow an expression of yours, Madame —

Boo.

Please.

ALICE.

You don't know what's going to be poop on ice, you don't know what's going to be a masterpiece.

Boo. (continued)

What?

GRIEVER. What is it, poop on ice?

Boo. I do not say that. She made that up, I swear. Tell them I do not say Poop on ice, please.

ALICE. You have to hear it first and see — hear how it sounds. I thought my last book was going to be one of the great tomes of Western literature; it turned out to be, what? Something like eighty-two pages . . .

GRIEVER. Poop? On ice?

Boo. I've never even met her, I swear to god.

TOM. I'm listening.

ALICE. Anyway, enough about me, what did *you* think of my last book? (*NORBERT crosses to the bar, takes a second beer.*)

Boo. I do not say poop on ice.

ALICE. No, she doesn't, I was just making that up. (*mouths*) She does. (*BOO sits on the floor with her back to the audience.*)

LIBBY. You know what scene in one of your books I love?

ALICE. No.

LIBBY. I love the scene where they're all sitting around—

GRIEVER. Take your hand away from your mouth.

LIBBY. Oh.

GRIEVER. We can't hear you.

LIBBY. It itches. Well, I love all your books, I really do.

GRIEVER. No, you were going to say which scene.

ALICE. Yes!

LIBBY. No, I don't know, I love all the scenes, I can't think of which one I meant, I can't.

ALICE. I was just getting excited.

LIBBY. I love them all, I really do.

ALICE. Well, you have good taste.

TOM. I haven't read any of your books, I'm sorry. (*LIBBY has crossed towards kitchen; GRIEVER takes her arm in passing.*)

	GRIEVER. (*mouthed, to LIBBY*)
ALICE. Oh, please, I'm always so surprised when one copy of one book sells. (*to BOO*) And don't you say one word.	You all right? . . . . You sure?
	(*LIBBY exits.*)

Boo. But you know what I always notice?

ALICE. What? What do you notice? Can I have a sip of your punch?

Boo. People don't relate to the words at all. It's as if — in anything, plays, books, movies — it's as if there was something behind the words.

ALICE. Intention. GRIEVER. Uh-huh?

Boo. Either behind the words or beyond the words —

ALICE. Intention.

Boo. May I say this?

ALICE. Sorry.

Boo. You got to make up your theory.

ALICE. You're absolutely right.

Boo. I mean . . . Eugene O'Neill, all right?

ALICE. Ugh.

Boo. But that's my point. There's something besides the words — beyond the words. (*NORBERT sits.*)

ALICE. Yes, but there's also —

Boo. Wait. Okay, O'Neill in one sense could not write.

TOM. *Eugene* O'Neill? (*LIBBY returns.*)

Boo. In one sense.

Really, go see them again, they're — his plays —

GRIEVER. The flowers look beautiful, don't they?

TOM. Uh-huh.

LIBBY. Mm-hm.

Boo. Very clunky and self-indulgent.

TOM. *Long Day's Journey Into Night?*

Boo. But they're not just about the words, that's what I'm trying to say. It's true, they appear to have been written by a seventh grader if you're just listening. But —

GRIEVER. The place looks great.

TOM. Didn't he win a

Boo. (*continued*) Yes, but—Obviously something transcends—

ALICE. Oh please, Knut Hamsen won the Nobel Prize, Herman Hesse!

TOM. I love Herman Hesse.

ALICE. *Steppenwolf?*

TOM. I love *Steppenwolf.*

ALICE. Well, as a teenager I did too, but have you gone back? I mean—

Boo. There's nothing wrong with that. I thought Thomas Wolf was the greatest writer who ever lived. Everything doesn't have to be for adults.

GRIEVER. I don't read and I'm proud of it.

Boo. A. E. Housman.

ALICE. Beatrix Potter.

Boo. Oh, Gore Vidal? Has—says that since we don't read anymore?

ALICE. When did we?

TOM. Uh-huh?

ALICE. (*to GRIEVER*) No offense.

Boo. Well, he says that too, but since we don't read anymore, since we got most of our information from television and movies—from images—

EMILY. Uh-huh?

Boo. That we lose the ability to think. Literally. Linearly. That's hard to say.

GRIEVER. Linearly.

Boo. That, in other words, across the page from left to right or top to bottom if you're Japanese or whatever it is—

GRIEVER. Mmmmmmmmm.

BOO. That thought is sequential. The logic is . . .

ALICE. Linear.

BOO. And if we grow up with movies and TV we lose the entire . . . Well, anyway, I think he's wrong, I do.

GRIEVER.	BOO.
Gore Vidal?	I think — Yes.
Wrong?	
I'm going to tell him you said that.	

BOO. (*crossing to bowl of mixed nuts*) I think philosophy and ideas — I think film and television are perfectly capable of conveying thought. I know you don't.

ALICE. You don't think that.

BOO. Why not?

GRIEVER. Can I get anybody anything — more punch there, Boo?

BOO. Yes, please, thanks. I love this.

ALICE. (*overlapping*) A word stands for something.

BOO. So does a picture.

ALICE.	GRIEVER.
I don't see how you can say that a succession of images —	Lib?
	Norb? You okay?
BOO. People talk in movies —	Anybody?

ALICE. Come on —

BOO. And they're sequential too, they're linear, you just can't go back and re-read.

ALICE. What does *La Dolce Vita* mean? What are the ideas? Your guess is as good as mine.

BOO. Oh, we're going to be in Italy in three

weeks and I've never been, GRIEVER.
I'm so excited. Really?   Libby was just there.
Is it beautiful?

LIBBY. Oh . . . (*turning her face front*) Very.

BOO. Oh, I want to hear all about it. All right, I'm
sorry, what does *La Dolce Vita* mean? Who knows, who
cares?

ALICE. That's my point exactly—

BOO. (*overlapping*) What does *The Penal Colony*
mean, what does *Moby Dick* mean?

ALICE. You can't—You're talking about fiction and
you're talking about thought, you can't. All fiction is
open to interpretation.

BOO. So is philosophy.

GRIEVER. (*with drinks*) She's got you there, Al.

BOO. Thanks.

ALICE. You can't make a movie out of Descarte.

BOO. Why not?

ALICE. His ideas?

BOO. Why not?

ALICE. Because. You can't.

BOO. Why not?

ALICE. Ideas do not come across in pictures, all right?

BOO. Why not?

ALICE. Ideas are not—   GRIEVER. I think you're
                              going to have to come up
                              with another argument.

ALICE. Words are ideas.

BOO. Pictures are ideas.

ALICE. They're not, they're pictures. They don't stand
for anything, they are the thing.

BOO. No, they're not, the thing is three-dimensional.

ALICE. You know what I'm saying, come on—

Boo. I think you're wrong. Buster Keaton falling off of a . . . what?

Griever. Train.

Boo. Thank you. Is a symbol. If you read that someone in a little porkpie hat falls off a train, why is that any more representative or less open to interpretation than the actual image of Buster Keaton falling off—It's more—open to interpretation than the visual, because you can't fill in the details, they're there. When I read the word "Train" I can have a thousand different trains, but Buster Keaton's train is one very specific train—

Griever. I love making a contribution. (*to LIBBY*) Do you want some help?

Libby. (*mouthed*) Excuse me. (*as she exits*) Nope.

Griever. You sure?

Libby. (*from off*) Yep, stay there.

Alice. I understand—

ALICE. But there's not the idea of train, that's my point; there's train and then there's Buster Keaton's train.

GRIEVER. (*sits on the floor*) Wait, I'm lost.

ALICE. Well, that's because you don't read.

GRIEVER. Right.

ALICE. (*jovial*) Anyway. (*She crosses to the bar, then sits by it.*)

GRIEVER. (*lighting a cigarette*) What do you do, Emily?

EMILY. I'm a secretary.

GRIEVER. Oh really? Where?

EMILY. Just a company.

GRIEVER. Uh-huh.

EMILY. Midtown.

GRIEVER.	ALICE.
What's it called?	What's it called?
(*to ALICE*) You owe me	
a coke.	

ALICE. All right.

EMILY. Um . . . I feel like I'm on the Merv Griffin show.

GRIEVER. Relax, honey, we're all pulling for you, everybody loves you.

EMILY. It's called Scientific Abstracts and I really hate talking about it on my day off.

GRIEVER. Okay.

BOO. (*overlapping*) Oh, here's to that, god almighty I hate thinking about work on Sunday. Let's talk about . . . I don't know. What shall we talk about?

TOM. What kind of work do you do? Oh, you just said . . .

BOO. That's all right. I'm a family therapist.

TOM. Oh.

Boo. (*She cracks up.*) I do family therapy . . . So.

EMILY. What's family therapy? (*BOO laughs again.*) Oh, you just said —

Boo. No, that's all right, that's all right. Family therapy. All right, you have a problem.

NORBERT. Okay.

Boo. You come to me. I would probably say, "This guy is past help." No, I'm tired, I'm sorry. Family therapy . . . Why can't I think of this?

ALICE. How much punch have you had?

Boo. I know this, I know this, this is what I do.

GRIEVER. Sure it is.

Boo. Family therapy. All right: say you're a drug addict.

NORBERT. I'm a drug addict.

Boo. That's funny, you don't look like a drug addict. No, really, really, I really do do this, doo-doo. I am bomb-o.

ALICE. I would say.

Boo. No, instead of treating you — instead of treating the problem as if you carry full responsibility —

NORBERT. Uh-huh.

Boo. And spending five years on the couch trying to analyze and understand all your wishes and your fears —

NORBERT. Right.

Boo. Which is fine. But expensive and long and painful and not always successful.

GRIEVER. But other than that, Mrs. Lincoln.

Boo. Really. We try to look at the dynamics of the family and see if . . . we can't blame somebody else for it. No, I'm sorry. Usually in a family structure there's one person who acts out — They drink or they flunk out in school —

NORBERT. Right.

Boo. Or they steal cars. But in my experience they are not necessarily the problem.

Norbert. They're the symptom.

Boo. Yes. So that often a child who supposedly has learning difficulties—

Norbert. Uh-huh.

Boo. Is really refusing to learn to read, say, because he knows damn well his father'll beat the shit out of him if he does.

Griever.
What?   Boo.
Learn to read.   Learn to read
Right.

Boo. The father can't read.

Griever. I gotcha.

Boo. So that's what I do.

Griever. Beat the shit out of 'em?

Boo. But I want to hear more about skydiving. I can't believe we're talking about family therapy. What's it like? Where do you do it? What's it cost? Where did you learn to do it? Why do you do it?

Griever. In that order.

Norbert. All right. Um, it's fun—that's why I do it. And Red Bank, New Jersey is where and I learned in the army.

Boo. Oh.

Norbert. And what else?

Griever. How much does it cost?

Norbert. Right. It costs about eighty dollars for your first day.

Boo. Oh, that's cheap.

Norbert. That includes five hours on the ground learning how to fall, how to land, how to fold your parachute, pull your ripcord.

ALICE. You don't actually jump out of the plane on your first day.

NORBERT. Sure.

ALICE. God. But you don't skydive on your first day.

NORBERT. Sure you do.

ALICE. But not free fall, I mean.

NORBERT. Sure you do.

BOO. Does Libby do that?

NORBERT. (*going for a cracker*) Well, we're having a little trouble getting Libby out of the plane. But — First we take you up on what's called a static line — you have a simulated ripcord, your chute opens automatically, then —

TOM. How high are you?

NORBERT. Right now?

TOM. Right.

BOO. Really

NORBERT. No, we start you at three thousand feet, that's the minimum and then —

BOO. Three thousand feet.

Right — And then we go up three hundred feet, increments of three hundred feet per jump; seventy-five hundred feet is about tops for a student jump.

BOO. How fast do you fall?

NORBERT. You start at sixty feet per second —

BOO. Start.

NORBERT. And you always open your chute at three thousand feet, so from seventy-five hundred feet you have a twenty-six second free fall; from twelve thousand feet which is your ceiling you have a seventy second free fall.

Boo. Jesus Christ.

EMILY. How many people forget to pull their ripcords?

NORBERT. Some, actually—

Boo. (*overlapping*) They do?

NORBERT. Well, sure. It's against your body's instincts to jump. I mean, you look out that blue window and you see the ground all the way down there and your gut says, No way, so sometimes—

GRIEVER. What do you do if they don't jump?

NORBERT. Push 'em. No, we go back and repeat the instructions. If after three or four days it looks like it's not going to happen, we refund your money.

Boo. That's nice.

NORBERT. You should all come out and try it. I'll give you a complimentary lessons. (*LIBBY re-enters.*)

ALICE. Food smells good, doesn't it? (*She crosses to coffee table, sits on the floor.*)

Boo. Now there's an offer.

GRIEVER. Food smells great, kiddo. . . . . . Tell 'em about Italy, come on.

ALICE. We're just hearing about your adventures. Norbert says you haven't quite gotten—

Boo. Oh, that's right, I want to hear about Italy, I want to hear about Italy. Is it gorgeous?

GRIEVER. (*to ALICE*) Sorry.

LIBBY. Oh, absolutely.

Boo. Oh god.

ALICE. Where did you stay?

LIBBY. You mean hotels?

ALICE. No, I meant what cities.

LIBBY. Oh . . .

GRIEVER. Venice.

LIBBY. Venice. And . . . I can't think.

ALICE. Well. Anywhere in Italy.

LIBBY. Sienna.

ALICE. Oh god, Sienna.

LIBBY. Mmmmmm.

ALICE. The light?

LIBBY. Wonderful.

GRIEVER. What is the matter with your mouth?

LIBBY. It itches, Griever.

GRIEVER. Sorry.

Boo. Well, I can't wait, I really can't. So far I can say . . . What?

ALICE. We've been on a crash course for the last three weeks.

Boo. Crash is right. Um—La mama . . . Una mama—

ALICE. La mia mama—

Boo.
La mia mama . . .   GRIEVER. Mama mia, that's a spicy speecy—

ALICE. All'—

Boo. All' aeroporto.   GRIEVER. Remember that? . . .

ALICE. Brava.   GRIEVER. . . . No?

Boo. La mia mama e all' aeroporto. My mother is at the airport.

GRIEVER. That should come in handy.

Boo. What else?

ALICE. Facciamo—

Boo. Facciamo—

ALICE. Un giro.

BOO. (*drops to her knees onto one of the pillows*) Facciamo un giro . . . Facciamo un giro . . . Facciamo—Shut up! Facciamo un giro . . .

GRIEVER. They'll starve to death before she can order a meal, but—no problem.

ALICE. In—

BOO. In mac china all'aeroporto.

ALICE. Vorrebbe guidare?

BOO. Si.

ALICE. No, come on.

BOO. Um . . .

TOM. Do you mind if I put on some music?

LIBBY. No.

TOM. I know where it is. (*He goes into the next room; EMILY follows him out.*)

BOO. Vorrebe . . . Vorrebbe . . . Christ—Mi . . . Mi . . .

GRIEVER. (*sings to the tune of "Volare."*) Vorrebbe! Whoa-ho-ho-ho!

ALICE. Piacerebbe.

BOO. Mi piacerebbe molto.

ALICE. Brava.

BOO. Mi piacerebbe molto. Alice speaks about seven languages fluently.

ALICE. That's not even remotely true but . . .

GRIEVER. Not me. I can barely speak English . . . Never travel . . .

BOO. I love what you've done with your apartment, Libby.

LIBBY. Thanks.

Boo. Do you entertain a lot?

LIBBY. (*lighting her and BOO's cigarettes*) No. Actually, this is the first time since I moved in.

Boo. Haven't you lived here. . . ? (*angular jazz piano music*)

LIBBY. Four years.

Boo. Oh. (*TOM and EMILY return to their positions on the sofa.*)

ALICE. What's this?

TOM. Cecil Taylor?

ALICE. Oh.

Boo. Who's that?

ALICE. Cecil Taylor? You've never heard of him?

Boo. Can I still stay at the party? Who's Cecil Taylor?

GRIEVER. He's very famous, Boo.

Boo. I gathered.

GRIEVER. I never heard of him either.

TOM. He's like the most technically proficient jazz pianist in the world.

Boo. Really?

TOM. Yeah, he literally alters the landscape of what you can do musically.

Boo. Really?

TOM. Yeah, he's real good.

Boo. Are you a musician?

TOM. Mm-hm.

LIBBY. Tom's a wonderful composer.

TOM. Oh, yeah, right—

LIBBY. You are.

TOM. No, I'm a studio musician. I do a lot of studio work.

Boo. Are you saying Libby lied to us, Tom?

TOM. But I don't know   LIBBY. (*mouthed*) He's
if you can hear it, but I   wonderful.
mean, he's literally re-

thinking what you can do
with melody. He's chang-
ing all the rules from the
ground up. He's taking
all your expectations and
kind of . . .

GRIEVER. I don't understand what you mean melody.
(*LIBBY gets up and heads for the kitchen.*)

TOM. Throwing them   GRIEVER. You want
back at you.   some help? (*to TOM*)
                            Sorry.

LIBBY. (*from off*) Nope.
GRIEVER. Are you sure?
LIBBY. Yep.
GRIEVER. I'm sorry.
TOM. Like a painter. He's breaking it up, you know,
and putting some parts of it in front of where they
belong and he's splitting up tonalities and colors,
shapes—
ALICE. Spitting up did you say?
TOM. Splitting.
ALICE. No, I know, I was . . .
TOM. He's literally challenging you to hear it, you
know, re-hear it. What is music?
GRIEVER. No, I know, but this isn't like a famous
melody? Or—?
TOM. Why not?
GRIEVER. I mean it isn't like "Raindrops on roses and
whiskers on kittens" backwards or something.
TOM. No . . .
GRIEVER. No, I know what you're saying. (*Pause.
They all listen.*) I know what you're saying. (*pause*) But
. . . (*pause*) Does anybody else get depressed on Sunday
nights?

Boo. Always.

Griever. I do.

Boo. I always get depressed.

Griever. I could be having the best time, I don't know what it is.

Alice. You don't always get depressed.

Boo. That's what I was feeling upstairs.

Alice. Still, you don't always get—

Boo. You know what it is? It's having to go to school in the morning.

Griever. Is that it?

Boo. I think so.   Alice. She doesn't
                                    always get depressed.

Boo. All right, I don't always get depressed.

Griever. I think it's Ed Sullivan.

Boo. Now that's interesting.

Griever. I think—No, you know what I think it is? I know what it is!

Boo. What?

Griever. I think it's Topo Gigio.

Boo. Who?

Griever. I really think it was Topo Gigio.

Alice. I remember Topo Gigio.

Griever. Right?

Alice. I loved Topo Gigio.

Griever. Really?

Alice. Yes, don't you remember?

Griever. You loved Topo Gigio?

Boo. Who's Topo Gigio?

Alice. Topo Gigio was this little mouse, Italian mouse—

Boo. Oh yes.

Alice. Remember?

Boo. Right, right.

ALICE. Topo Gigio, I loved Topo Gigio.

BOO. You loved Topo Gigio?

ALICE. Yes. Is that like Lawrence Welk or something? I thought he was cute.

BOO. He was.

GRIEVER. He was cute.

ALICE. I want to die all of a sudden. I don't know what it is. I loved—Yes, I loved Topo Gigio, take me away.

GRIEVER. Anyway—

ALICE. (*to EMILY*) Do you remember Topo Gigio?

EMILY. Mm-hm.

ALICE. You do. Did you like him? (*shakes her head no*) God.

GRIEVER. Anyway, you know, he was always going "Eddie! I love you Eddie! Kiss me!"

BOO. That's very good.

ALICE. (*to TOM*) Did you hate him too? (*He did.*) Everybody. No wonder you get depressed on Sundays. I will too from now on. Forever and and ever. (*crosses to bar unit*)

GRIEVER. Right? I just remember he was the last thing on the show and he come on . . . Maybe you're right, maybe it's because I knew I had to go to bed. But I just remember this tremendous feeling of sadness. Emptiness. I think

BOO. Shhhh!

BOO. (*to GRIEVER*) Uh-huh?

that's why I
never wanted to
go to Italy.

ALICE. Because of Topo Gigio? Oh come on.

Boo. (*to TOM*) Can
we turn this down? I like
it, it's just . . . It's not
really party music. (*TOM
exits; BOO calls from door-
way.*) Don't turn it all the
way off.

NORBERT. I liked him.

GRIEVER. Can I get any-
body anything? Boober?

ALICE. You did?
Would you say that again?
Wait. (*ALICE crosses up
to sofa unit. EMILY
moves to sofa, sits on
floor, facing the audi-
ence.*) Excuse me, Dr.
Weinstein? . . . Doctor?

Boo. No thanks.

Boo. What?

GRIEVER. Tom? . . .
Anybody?

(*GRIEVER stands in door-
way to kitchen; turntable
revolves, revealing a por-
tion of the kitchen; LIBBY
stands, arms folded.
Lights dim on the party
sequence as TOM returns
to his permanent position
on the sofa. EMILY has
crossed to the coffee
table, sits, facing the audience. Throughout the
next dialogue we see the
party, silhouetted, sound-
lessly enacted.*)

ALICE. He liked Topo
Gigio.

Boo. Well sure he did,
he was probably two years
old.

ALICE. Don't pay any
attention to her. She's trying to take Topo Gigio
away from us. Topo Gigio
is immortal.

GRIEVER. Congratulations, it's going great, don't you think? Everybody's having a good time, no fights. What's the matter? Am I being a jerk? My hair look stupid? What? Just tell me. I fucked up. (*LIBBY smiles broadly: no tooth.*)

LIBBY. What do you think? Nice? I was going to do all of them, but I wanted to see how one looked first. I don't know, I can't decide.

GRIEVER. What did you do?

LIBBY. Do you think I'll be more successful on dates or what?

GRIEVER. What did you do?

LIBBY. I thought I was doing an incredible job, subtly hiding the fact that I look like Margaret Hamilton and every two seconds you keep asking me what is the matter with my mouth.

GRIEVER. Well, honey pie—

LIBBY. (*not stopping*) Because someone who was supposed to come early and help with the food didn't so I had to do everything by myself which is why I look like Margaret Hamilton.

GRIEVER. Dueling guilt trips—

LIBBY. And now the only thing that would make me happy would be for you to go back out there and be charming until everyone goes home and we can—

GRIEVER. Baby—

LIBBY. (*continuous*) Begin to forget this whole hideous experience and someday maybe someday—

GRIEVER. Sugar butt—

LIBBY. (*continuous*) We might be able to pick up the shattered remains of our friendship and see what we might be able to—

GRIEVER. Liver lips—

LIBBY. (*continuous*) Piece together over a drink if I'm

in a good mood.

GRIEVER. First of all, Margaret Hamilton had all her teeth.

LIBBY. I'm so happy this amuses you.

GRIEVER. Second of all, you look fine, nobody notices, nobody would care, and it's cute. Let me see it again.

LIBBY. Why are you allowed to live?

GRIEVER. Let me see. Please?

LIBBY. If you say one word to anybody—

GRIEVER. Say cheese! Now how did we do this?

LIBBY. I was taking the lid off a caviar jar.

GRIEVER. And this is a cap, not a tooth.

LIBBY. This was a cap.

GRIEVER. This was a cap. So this does not hurt physically.

LIBBY. Spiritually.

GRIEVER. Now. You are not going to spend the rest of the evening grunting everytime someone asks you a question.

LIBBY. I can if I want to.

GRIEVER. That's right, it's your party—

LIBBY. And I'll cry if I want to, it isn't funny.

GRIEVER. Maybe a little bit.

LIBBY. The whole thing was a horrible idea, I don't know anybody anymore, I didn't know who to invite . . .

GRIEVER. Everyone is having a great time—

LIBBY. I wasn't ready, Griever, I was not ready to do this.

GRIEVER. Yes you were.

| LIBBY. Everybody knows. | GRIEVER. They don't know. |
| It's the wrong chemistry, | Now look at me . . . . . . |

nobody likes anybody, the . . . . Stop . . .
food isn't ready and I
look like a witch.

GRIEVER. Nobody knows anything, what if they did?

LIBBY. I'm not talking about the tooth.

GRIEVER. What if everybody knew everything? Well?
What if they did? Tom knows. I know. We love you.

LIBBY. I can't—(*He tries to embrace her.*) Don't hold
me. I'm sorry.

GRIEVER. It's all right.

LIBBY. Go say I'm having trouble with the sauce,
don't let anybody in here.

GRIEVER. We can talk about this whole thing in
group, all right?

LIBBY. I'm fine.

GRIEVER. You can tell everybody how horrible I was
at your party.

LIBBY. Fine.

GRIEVER. I'm real proud of you, you know that. And
you can't even notice it, all right, I lied.

LIBBY. Go!

(*Turntable begins to revolve, lights and sound slowly up
on the party scene as LIBBY disappears.*)

GRIEVER. And I love you, don't forget that.

LIBBY. I'd rather have a big bag of money.

NORBERT. The army is very weird, though. I mean, it's not like the real world.

TOM. Right.

ALICE. I'm tired, aren't you?

BOO. No, I just want to eat something before I turn into a pineapple.

GRIEVER.
What happened
to Cecil Beaton?

NORBERT. You
pretty much
have to put your
disbelief in
suspension or
whatever the—

ALICE. We
bullied him into
turning it off.

GRIEVER. (*to NORBERT who is smoking a joint*)
You're taking drugs, aren't you? I leave you alone for
two seconds, give me that. (*takes joint, takes long drag
on it*)

BOO. Can we do anything to help?

GRIEVER. I wouldn't suggest going in there if I were
you?

ALICE AND BOO. Why?

ALICE. You owe me a coke!

GRIEVER. Then you owe it to me.

ALICE. Right.

GRIEVER. Libby, or Elizabeth as she is known to
almost no one, is probably the world's most phenome-
nal control freak when it comes to cooking.

BOO. Ah.

GRIEVER. (*to NORBERT*) Do you want this back?
Can't have it. All right.

NORBERT. Ha-ha-ha.

GRIEVER. No, seriously, she'll break your legs if you
go in there.

BOO. Oh I like a girl like that, don't you?

ALICE. Mmmm.

NORBERT. (*Hands joint to EMILY. Piano music has
appeared underneath this scene.*) Emily.

GRIEVER. All right, I have a question for ze doctor.

EMILY. Thanks.
Boo. Hm?
GRIEVER. All right . . . (*EMILY hands joint to ALICE.*)
ALICE. Thanks.

(*A pin-spot has slowly come up on EMILY's face. All the other characters freeze and EMILY sings to the piano accompaniment.*)

EMILY.
"They all want the same thing.
My mother'd been through it.
She told me to remember
They all want the same thing.
My father left her.
She had to raise me by herself.
After going out a few times
She gave up on replacements.
Look around you.
Look at your sister.
Where did she find that guy?
Someday soon he'll leave her.
Just like your father
He went to California.
He didn't even leave me
For some other women."

(*The other characters unfreeze momentarily; EMILY crosses up of them. The piano vamps continue beneath dialogue.*)

GRIEVER. The unconscious.
Boo. Yes?

GRIEVER. The human being's unconscious?

Boo. Yes?

GRIEVER. All right. I have been in therapy for about seventy five years. (*freeze*)

EMILY. (*sings*)
"I came to the city
To get away from mother.
Some of you others
Are here for the same reason.
Worked as a file clerk.
Met a man and fell in love.
He told me he was married.
I thought it didn't matter.
We took an apartment.
Lived there for nearly half a year.
He said he'd divorce his wife.
I couldn't tell my mother.
One night I left him,
Left him in that apartment.
All my books and records,
Well, I suppose they're still there."
(*Unfreeze. Vamp continues.*)

GRIEVER. And—

ALICE. You're going to have a breakthrough any day now.

GRIEVER. Thanks. No, I really have thought about this. Do. . . ? (*Freeze. EMILY has crossed up of GRIEVER.*)

EMILY. (*sings*)
"Uptown
Found a place with two roommates.
We all work in offices.
I found a new boyfriend.

Some weekends
He takes me to the country
Where he gives his wild parties.
Those nights I sleep alone.
And I'm weary,
Tired of turning on
With so many people
With nothing in their faces.
From California
To Mississippi
Everybody's looking
For just the same thing."
(*Unfreeze. Music slowly fades out under dialogue.*)

GRIEVER. Do patients—? What am I trying to say? Does everybody—? Everybody has an unconscious.

ALICE. Presumably.

GRIEVER. Does everybody have the same—(*to EMILY*) This is going to sound so stupid—(*to BOO*) Basically the same kinds of—

BOO. Yes, I think so. (*EMILY sits downstage of coffee table.*)

ALICE. He hasn't even asked the question.

BOO. I know. I think I know what he's getting at—

GRIEVER. I mean, I see people on the street, all right?

BOO. Uh-huh?

GRIEVER. Politicians.

BOO. Yes, I think it's natural to wonder about— And I think the answer is yes.

ALICE. To what? What's the question?

BOO. People's basic fears and basic inner mechanisms are the same, is that what you're asking?

GRIEVER. Yeah.

ALICE. But you don't know that.

GRIEVER. Sort of. Is it? I don't know.

BOO. No, I don't. He asked what I thought. I think the difference between people are superficial and—

BOO. Basically—Basically we're all cut from the same cloth.

ALICE. But—. . . What was I just reading? . . . God, it was this incredible quote . . . This is— this is exactly what it was about . . . What the fuck was that—?

GRIEVER. All right, but . . . I mean, okay, why does somebody become a Nazi?

BOO. Well, it's—I mean, the Marxists—

GRIEVER. Right—

BOO. (*continuous*) Say it's economic, the Freudians say it's because the Germans toilet train their kids too soon.

GRIEVER. Right, the whole tie between—

BOO. Sadism—

GRIEVER. Right.

TOM. Because they what?

BOO. They toilet train their kids too soon.

TOM. So they killed six million jews?

ALICE. But—May I say something? I don't see—I mean, a child's experience isn't the same as an adult's. A woman's—I don't know what a penis feels like.

BOO. It's really not as stupid as it sounds—

BOO. That's not the question.

ALICE. I mean, I know what one feels like, but—Why do we have to have I'm-the-same-as-you, you're-the-same-as-me? Why does one person scream when they get a hangnail and another person not even flinch when they get—

GRIEVER. Alice! Alice, Alice, Alice.

BOO. Because. You know why.

ALICE. Why?

BOO. Because they're sissies.

NORBERT. Okay. Did you ever wonder—as a kid—if what you saw as the color blue—

ALICE. Yes!

NORBERT. And what other people saw as the color blue was really like two different colors?

ALICE. Yes, that's what I'm saying!

BOO. But it's not.

ALICE. You don't know that.

BOO. I do know it. Physiologically it's the same.

ALICE. But you're not inside his experience.

BOO. True, I am deducing it's the same.

ALICE. Empirically?

BOO. Not empirically.

ALICE. (*not stopping, to EMILY*) I have no idea what that word means, do you? No, you can go sit where Norbert sits, but you won't see what Norbet sees.

GRIEVER. Well, Norbert won't see anything if she's sitting in his lap—

ALICE. (*overlapping the last few words*) No, all right, if this were a play?

Boo. (*overlapping the last words of ALICE's*) May I just interject something here?.

ALICE. What?

Boo. I really love this punch.

ALICE. Good.

Boo. I would like to get in the bowl and go for a swim.

ALICE. If this were a play or a novel?

EMILY. Uh-huh?

ALICE.
You have the whole web of connections: how you know Libby and why you're here and what I know about you and what you know about me, but even if you could graph it all out?

Boo. (*crossing to the bar*) I would like to have a relationship with this punch . . . Raise little baby punch bowls . . .

GRIEVER. Thank you for sharing that . . .

NORBERT. Yeah?

ALICE. Even if you could put all the different pieces of the puzzle together, your piece and my piece and—

GRIEVER. Watch it, Al.

ALICE. Right. And what you want and why you say what you say or don't say and what's going on in the kitchen and what you did this afternoon and what I'm going to do when I get home and what he's thinking—Even if you could assemble all these little pieces of the puzzle—

GRIEVER. Right.

ALICE. From all the different angles so they all fit together perfectly . . .

EMILY. Uh-huh?

ALICE. You would still have . . . a puzzle. (*no reaction*) I thought that was so brilliant. (*LIBBY has just entered.*)

LIBBY. Food's almost ready.

ALICE. All right, here's Libby.

GRIEVER. Heeeeeeeeeeeeeeeeeeere's Libby!

(*GRIEVER, TOM and BOO all sing the Johnny Carson theme. ALICE barrels ahead.*)

ALICE. All right, I promise I'll shut up as soon as I finish this. Do you mind my using you as an example?

LIBBY. No.

ALICE. Even if you could ascertain why Libby — wants to go skydiving or why she had us all here for dinner or why, I don't know, she wears her hair like that or why her lip itches, you still couldn't — (*GRIEVER has stifled a laugh.*) What?

LIBBY. Nothing.

ALICE. You still couldn't feel the itch.

GRIEVER. Oh go ahead, tell 'em.

LIBBY. (*under her breath*) Griever!   ALICE. The defense rests, I'm sorry.

GRIEVER. Go on.

ALICE. What?

GRIEVER. Nobody cares.

ALICE. What?

LIBBY. I don't want to.

GRIEVER. You're being silly.

LIBBY. That's my perogative, isn't it? (*Long pause. Everyone stares at her. At last she give in, smiles a big toothy grin.*) Hi.

(*Lights dim to scene change light; at the same time so-*

prano aria from Puccini's "La Rondine" is heard, full volume. The black sculptural pieces are again rearranged by the actors, this time all facing full front. ALICE and BOO will be C. stage. LIBBY and NORBERT stage R. TOM and EMILY stage L. GRIEVER alone US., his back to the audience.)

SCENE 3

(LIBBY and NORBERT are clearing away dishes. GRIEVER sits motionless, alone. EMILY, wearing TOM's long shirt and nothing else, is eating popcorn and watching television, the sound turned off. ALICE and BOO, C., are listening to the aria out of the scene change. Deep violet light against the scrim, visible through the window/canvas.)

SOPRANO. (*singing*) "Folle amore! Folle ebrazza! Chi la sottil carezza d'un bacio cosi ardente mai ridi potra!"
ALICE. Listen.
SOPRANO. "Ah! mio sogno!"
ALICE. (*spoken*) Ah! my soul!
SOPRANO. "Ah! mia vita!"
ALICE. Ah! My life!
SOPRANO. "Che importa la richezza se alfine e rigiorita le felicita O sogno d'or poter amar . . ."
BOO. It's beautiful.

(She puts on her headphones and resumes language lesson from Scene One. ALICE gets up and turns off the music, offstage. LIBBY enters.)

LIBBY. (*to NORBERT, carrying dirty dishes*) Oh, just leave those.

NORBERT. I don't mind.

LIBBY. All right. (*NORBERT exits with dishes; LIBBY sits.*)

TOM. (*entering, shirt open*) Fucking dykes, you know?

ALICE. (*re-entering*)
Everybody seemed nice, I thought.

TOM. The trouble with Shakespeare, of course, is the same thing that's wrong with Beethoven and Bach, basically . . . Ya-da Ya-da . . .

BOO. What?

ALICE. Oh, sorry.

BOO. No, say.

ALICE. I said I thought everybody seemed nice, didn't you?

BOO. Mmmmm.

ALICE. You don't have to use the headphones.

BOO. No, they help.

ALICE. Oh.

TOM. Turn the sound up.

EMILY. No, I like to try to figure out what they're saying.

TOM. Yeah? Make up stories? I used to do that when I was a kid. Sneak down and watch TV at night without the sound, try to imagine what the story was. Give everybody names. (*NORBERT re-enters.*) And then something would happen in the story that didn't make sense with what I'd already decided and I'd have to shift everything around. Re-adjust my prejudices. My alliances.

EMILY. Uh-huh.

NORBERT. Do you want to be alone or something?

LIBBY. No, actually, I don't.

ALICE. I'm tired.

NORBERT. All right. (*NORBERT exits with more dishes.*)

ALICE. Do you mind if I put my head in your lap? (*She*

does.) Mmmmmmm. (*pause*) Montagne.

BOO. Hm?

ALICE. Montagne.

BOO. What do I say?

ALICE. I don't know.

TOM. . . . Fucking song . . . (*picks up his sheet music, resumes work*)

BOO. Montagne.

ALICE. Montagne.

BOO. Montagne.

LIBBY. (*calling offstage*) That's enough.

BOO. Montagne.

NORBERT. (*re-entering*) I just want you to know I'm a world-reknowned, championship dishwasher.

LIBBY. Well, I don't care, Norbert, I want you to sit down right now and be nice to me.

NORBERT. Do I have to?

TOM. I mean, I know—I *know* I can write it, I just can't write it. You know?

NORBERT. So.

TOM. I know just what it should be, I can hear it.

NORBERT. Tell me about yourself . . .

TOM. (*continued*) I can feel what the words are, I just can't . . .

NORBERT. How's that for a first line?

TOM. (*very soft*) It's like one of those fucking jingles that goes around in your head, you know?

EMILY. Uh-huh?

LIBBY. Well . . . I have no tooth.

NORBERT. Uh-huh?

LIBBY. And beyond that . . .

TOM. I just can't . . . I almost asked everybody to shut up for a second, I was like afraid I was going to lose it.

EMILY. What, at the party?

NORBERT. So who were all these people?

LIBBY. Tonight? You know, Norb?

TOM. (*looking at sheet music*) I don't know . . .

LIBBY. I really don't know.

TOM. I don't know about the middle part.

LIBBY. I really don't.

NORBERT. Weren't they your friends?

TOM. Which sounds better? (*He picks up the guitar, plays.*)

NORBERT. What?   ALICE. What?

BOO. Hm?

ALICE. What are you thinking?

LIBBY. I'm not being very good company, am I?

BOO. What do you sup-   NORBERT. It's okay.
pose Libby's story is?   LIBBY. Is it?

ALICE. She's straight,
I'm sure.

BOO. Nooooooo.

LIBBY. I'm glad.

ALICE. Oh, I don't know, what do you mean? . . .
You have that look on your face.

LIBBY. I like you.

BOO. I don't know . . .

NORBERT. I like you too.

BOO. I can't put my finger on it.

ALICE. Did you want to put your finger on it? What
about Griever, is he straight?

BOO. Why does every-
thing always have to come   ALICE. It doesn't — It
back to us?   doesn't, I'm just curious.

TOM. Or. (*plays another version of the same phrase*)

LIBBY. Music?

ALICE. What about Emily?

BOO. She's straight.

LIBBY. Or something to drink?

Boo. No, I liked her.

ALICE. You did?   LIBBY. Easy to please, aren't you?

Boo. Mm-hm.

ALICE. Me too. Maybe a little bimbotic, but . . .

Boo. What?

ALICE. Bimbotic? The adjectival form of bimbo?

Boo. Bimbotic?

ALICE. You like that?   TOM. Wait, I'll play 'em again. (*He does.*)

Boo. Did you make that up?

ALICE. I don't know. Maybe.

Boo. You don't know if you made it up?

NORBERT. Can I ask you something?

LIBBY. Sure.

NORBERT. It's none of my business, but . . . Are you and Griever — ?

LIBBY. Oh. No. Sort of. Who knows?

NORBERT. Uh-huh.

TOM. That's one, all right?

LIBBY. I don't know what we are. He's helped me a lot, and I love him, but . . . It's not really — I'm not really ready. He is. I'm not. I'd like to be.

NORBERT. Uh-huh.

LIBBY. Not necessarily for Griever. I don't know what I mean. Sorry.

NORBERT. That's okay.

TOM. (*finishes playing*) That's the other one. What do you think?

EMILY. Well. They sound sort of the same. Sorry.

LIBBY. Sorry.

ALICE. (*sitting up*) Sorry.

NORBERT. No.

Boo. What's the matter?

ALICE. I drank too much.

Boo. What?

ALICE. (*exiting*) I drank too much.

(*GRIEVER has gotten up and dialed his phone. LIBBY's phone rings. She looks at it. It rings again.*)

NORBERT. You want me to get it? (*LIBBY shakes her head, goes to phone, answers.*)

LIBBY. Hi.

GRIEVER. Congratulations, congratulations!

LIBBY. Thanks.

GRIEVER. (*singing*) Bum-ba-bum-bum-bum-bum-bum!

LIBBY. Thanks.

GRIEVER. You did it!

LIBBY. Wellll—

GRIEVER. You did, come on.

LIBBY. Yeah. Everybody left kind of early.

GRIEVER. Early? It's eleven o'clock on Sunday night.

LIBBY. Yeah, I know.

GRIEVER. It was terrific, it really was. I'm real proud of you. You're over the hump.

LIBBY. I guess.

GRIEVER. You are. I think it was terrific, I really do. Alice is a stitch, isn't she?

LIBBY. Isn't she?

GRIEVER. And Boo? Tom seemed to have a good time.

LIBBY. Oh good, I couldn't tell.

GRIEVER. You by yourself?

LIBBY. You should have stayed, you just flew out the door.

GRIEVER. I know, I know.

LIBBY. You home?

GRIEVER. Is Norbert still there?

LIBBY. We were just sitting and talking a bit—

GRIEVER. Uh-huh.

LIBBY. Relaxing. Did you get a cab?

GRIEVER. Oh yeah, no problem, but listen, I'll let you go.

LIBBY. Please don't—

GRIEVER. No, I'm a jerk.

LIBBY. You're not a jerk, you're terrific.

GRIEVER. I'll see you in group, all right? (*He hangs up, takes his phone off the hook.*)

LIBBY. Grieve? (*to NORBERT*) I'll just be a second. (*She dials, listens, hangs up.*)

NORBERT. Listen, maybe . . .

LIBBY. No, please, I like having you here. Please stay.

NORBERT. Okay. (*They sit.*)

LIBBY. Oh, Norbert.

NORBERT. What?

LIBBY. You're so sweet and you have such a stupid name.

NORBERT. Thanks.

LIBBY. I don't know.

NORBERT. Well first thing, we've got to get you a dentist. (*LIBBY laughs hysterically.*) What? . . . What? . . . (*He laugh goes on and on, verging on the hysterical.*)

LIBBY. I'm sorry.

NORBERT. What did I say? (*She looks as if she may be crying.*) Hey.

LIBBY. Oh god.

NORBERT. Hey.

LIBBY. I'm sorry.

NORBERT. Don't be sorry. I'm right here.

LIBBY. Oh . . .

NORBERT. Come on.

LIBBY. I can't, I'm sorry.

NORBERT. That's okay.

LIBBY. No, it's not you.

NORBERT. I know.

BOO. (*Having taken off her headphones, she calls to offstage.*) Are you all right?

LIBBY. I'm sorry.

BOO. Baby?

ALICE. (*from off*) I'm fine, I'm sitting on the pot.

BOO. All right.

NORBERT. All right?

TOM. What's happening?

EMILY. (*staring at the television*) I can't tell yet. Somebody's trying to get something from somebody.

TOM. Like what?

EMILY. I can't tell. You have to watch.

LIBBY. . . . When I first came to New York?

NORBERT. Uh-huh?

(*GRIEVER, who has remained standing, smoking a cigarette, now places the receiver back in its cradle and sits on the back of his armchair, his back to the audience. BOO has laid on her side, resting on her elbow. TOM continues work on his song. EMILY never takes her eyes off the television screen.*)

LIBBY. I didn't know a soul, you know? I didn't know why I was here or what I was going to do. I just came.

NORBERT. Uh-huh.

LIBBY. And I ran into Tom on the street.

NORBERT. Uh-huh.

LIBBY. It was nice, you know, to see a familiar face even though we weren't all that close in high school. And we started messing around. Nothing serious, it was never anything serious . . . Then I went to get my teeth cleaned, of all things. I had thirteen cavities, so I wound up . . . seeing a lot of . . .

NORBERT. The—

LIBBY. The dentist. Right. You got it. And . . . Martin Vanderhoffer.

NORBERT. Uh-huh.

LIBBY. And he was just a lot of fun. His family had a lot of money. I mean, a lot a lot of money, so he didn't have to work at all if he didn't want to, but he liked to which I liked. And he was fun.

NORBERT. Uh-huh.

LIBBY. And so we started to go out. And I didn't see Tom much. At all. And I got more involved with Marty. We talked about getting married . . .

ALICE. (*from off*) I know what I wanted to show you. Boo. What?

ALICE. I remembered what I wanted to show you, if I can find it.

Boo. What?

LIBBY. (*overlapping*) Aaaaand we did. Get married.

NORBERT. Uh-huh.

LIBBY. Big wedding. And . . . we laughed. Marty . . . We bought a big apartment on East 71st Street—much too big for just the two of us. Brand new building, we had a terrace and windows on three sides. It was almost the penthouse. We'd been married about three months— not quite—And . . . I think I was pregnant. I was. We talked about it and I was late. Anyway, I could have been . . . And we were standing by the window. I didn't

have any clothes on. I was looking out. It was late—
Late afternoon. Everything was blue—as blue as it can
be before it gets black.

NORBERT. Uh-huh?

LIBBY. And Marty said, Come out on the terrace. I
said, I don't have any clothes on. And he brought me
this little robe. And we walked out on the terrace. (*BOO
puts her hand over her eyes as if she has a headache.*)
We'd only lived there two months. And he kissed me
and I put my head back to look up at the sky. Our re-
flections were in the glass. And I put my head back; we
lived on the seventh floor, there was another one above
us. (*GRIEVER puts his head back as if sighing.*) And
we leaned—he leaned—I set my back against the rail
and it . . . just . . . We were gone; we were over. I saw us
leave the window. I looked—past him, my hands reached
past him to try to hold something, there wasn't anything
. . . just blue . . . And I didn't black out. I thought—very
clearly . . . This is bad. This is real. And it's true, you see
everything pass before your eyes. Everything. Slowly,
like a dream, and Marty was . . . Marty was climbing up
me and screaming and we turned . . . over . . . once . . .
and . . . we went through an awning . . . Sloan's . . .
Which saved my life . . . And I broke every bone in my
face. I have a completely new face. My teeth were all
shattered; these are all caps.

ALICE. (*from off*) Now I know this is here because I
just saw it.

BOO. What?

ALICE. Wait.

LIBBY. I was in traction for ten months. And Tom
came to see me every week. Every day sometimes.
Marty's family. Who sued the building. I mean, they
never even attached it to the wall. It wasn't even attached. It was just a rail—a loose rail. There was

another one on another floor, the same thing could have happened . . . I landed on him. I killed him. I can't— (*NORBERT moves towards her; she flinches.*) It's seven years. I'm thirty-three years old. I can't have anybody hold me. I can never be held. (*pause*)

NORBERT. I'm going to stay here, all right? . . . I won't hold you . . . (*ALICE comes on with a book.*)

BOO. What is this?

ALICE. (*reading*) "There is, let us confess it . . ." Wait. (*She sits next to BOO who is sitting up again.*)

BOO. Who is this?

ALICE. "About sympathy—" All right, just listen.

NORBERT. All right?

ALICE. (*reading*) "About sympathy, for example. We can do without it. That illusion of a world so shaped that it echoes every groan, of human beings so tied together by common needs and fears that a twitch at one wrist jerks another, where however strange your experience other people have had it too, where however far you travel in your own mind a someone has been there before you—is all an illusion."

BOO. Who is this?

ALICE. "We do not know our own souls, let alone the souls of others. Human beings do not go hand in hand the whole stretch of the way. There is a virgin forest in each; a snowfield where even the print of birds' feet is unknown." . . . Collected Essays, Volume Four, V. Woolf. (*She puts down the book.*) What's the matter?

NORBERT. It's going to be all right.

BOO. Do you even love me?

ALICE. Of course I love you. Honey. I love you so very much, you know that. (*GRIEVER dials LIBBY's number and hangs up before it can ring.*)

BOO. You know, if you'd said "I love you so much" or

"I love you very much" but you love me "so very much?"

ALICE. What's wrong with that?

BOO. What is that? Who is that for?

ALICE. I don't understand, I really don't.

BOO. I think you're more in love with the sound of your own voice than you are with me is what I think.

ALICE. Why? Because I read a passage from Virginia Woolf?

BOO. (*overlapping*) If you want to know what I think—Because you have to be right, Alice. You have to, have to, have to be right. Always. Always, Alice. It's like you don't think I have a brain in my head.

ALICE. I think you're one of the smartest people I ever met in my life.

BOO. (*overlapping*) But you don't. It's like you made me up in your head. Oh, Alice's lover is a doctor. Isn't that interesting? Isn't that flattering? To Alice.

TOM. This fucking . . .

BOO. (*overlapping*)
You ask me questions about thinks I know about—Science—and then you answer your own question. Incorrectly.

TOM. . . . I know what it is . . . I know it . . .

ALICE. What are we talking about? The corpus callosum? I was just so pleased I remembered.

BOO. You're always so pleased. You're always so pleased with yourself.

ALICE. Well, what? Empirical? I was playing—

BOO. (*overlapping*) It's not that.

ALICE. Honey, I absolutely adore you and if I'm not communicating it—

BOO. (*overlapping*) It's not that.

Tom. That's it. All right.

Alice. Then tell me what it is, all right? (*GRIEVER dials.*)

Tom. All *right*.

Alice. What? . . . Please. (*LIBBY's phone rings.*)

Boo. I miss . . . (*ring*)

Norbert. I'll get it.

Tom. I got it. Finally.

Norbert. (*after the second ring*) Hello?

Alice. What?

Norbert. Hello?

Boo. I miss us. (*GRIEVER hangs up.*)

Alice. Us?

Norbert. Hung up.

Boo. I miss our time together.

Alice. We're going away in three weeks.

Boo. I miss . . . The first time you made love to me? I felt like a baby being born. (*TOM plays the guitar, softly.*) And now . . . I'll never forget when you first touched me.

Tom. (*to EMILY who has switched off the TV and is staring into space*) You all right?

Boo. At Carl's? I'll never forget that feeling.

Emily. You know what I wish?

Boo. Oh my god. Fall-ing in love with you? November? And moving in here with you. And now I'm always on call. And your damn book, I hate that book, I do.

Tom. Wait, baby, I'm almost finished.

Alice. I know.

Boo. I do. I don't care what you call it, pick something. Call it Poop On Ice. I'm tired of hearing lit-tle bits of it and should his name be Frank or should it

be Franklin? I listen to people all day long, I listen to
their problems, I listen to their little—

TOM. I've almost got it.

BOO. (*not stopping*) Niggling fucking complaints
about nothing—

ALICE. I know, I know—

BOO. (*not stopping*) And none of them ever gets any
better.

ALICE. That's not true.

BOO. And it's not going to be any better even if I start
a private practice, it's always going to be other people's
problems as long as I live.

ALICE. That's the work you chose.

TOM. (*sings*) "From California to Mississippi . . ."
Mmmm. (*finishes the song, satisfied*) All right, what do
you wish?

LIBBY. I wish . . .

EMILY. I wish everybody had a little window. Right in
front like a TV screen?

LIBBY. Sometimes I wish . . .

TOM. A window?

EMILY. You know. Like just a little window where
you could see in and see what they were feeling and
thinking about.

LIBBY. I don't know . . .

EMILY. So you wouldn't always have to wonder. You
could just see. Wouldn't that be neat?

LIBBY. We would be by the window. You know? And
Marty would say, Come out on the terrace. And I'd say
. . . No. Let's stay here.

ALICE. Baby.

LIBBY. It's so blue.

ALICE. I'm here.

LIBBY. All right?

TOM. Well, I wish we had a piano is what I wish.

LIBBY. Oh god.

NORBERT. It's all right.

TOM. You know?

LIBBY. God.

NORBERT. It's all right.

TOM. Big . . . black . . . baby grand . . . Sit her in the window?

BOO. I wish we were there right now.

TOM. All that light?

BOO. I do.

TOM. Blue light? You know?

BOO. I just want to walk on the Grand Canal with you.

TOM. Cold . . . white . . . keys . . .

BOO. And hold your hand.

TOM. Smooth, clean.

BOO. (*beginning to overlap*) And make love to you.

TOM. God.

ALICE. Cara mia.

BOO. I do.

TOM. I can just feel it.

ALICE. Come la nascita d'una bambina.

BOO. What's that?

ALICE. Like a baby being born.

(*As they all begin to speak together, no voice can take more importance than another. They are all quiet and distinct — taking their time.*)

LIBBY. We would just be by the   EMILY. I really do . . .   BOO. I

window . . .
And I would
say . . . stay
with me here
. . . It's so
blue . . . Stay
here . . .

And you
could crawl
right in. Like
. . . if every-
one was made
of glass. I
would love
that . . .

wish we were
there . . .
Right now
. . . And I
could fall in
love with you
again—All
over again,
but this time
in Venice—

Tom. Just
touch the
keys, you
know?
And—

(*TOM reaches forward as if to play the piano. He presses his finger down and we hear music—the song he has been trying to write, the same song EMILY sang—her piano accompaniment, very soft at first.*)

Tom. *Damn!*
Norbert. I know.

Libby. And
we would just
. . . We would
just float away
. . . .
. . . . We
would become
the blue . . .
. . . . . . Just the
two of us . . .
. . . . . . You
know? . . . . . .
Right through
the glass . . .

Emily. If you
could just
open up the win-
dow and crawl
in . . .

(*GRIEVER sways to the music very gently.*)

Emily. I do
. . . I wish every-
one was made of
glass. And I
wish everybody

Alice. Ti
adoro.

Boo. And we
could look in all
the windows . . .
Hold hands . . .
Everything'll be
blue . . .

Alice. Ti
amo.

Boo. And
we'll ride in a

| We would just . . . Float . . . away . . . . . . Right through the glass . . . | had a little window. Don't you? . . . I do . . . | gondola? And we'll just float away . . . |

ALICE. Come la nascita d'una bambina . . .

Boo. Okay? We'll just . . . float away . . .

LIBBY. Forever . . .

(The music becomes rhapsodic. GRIEVER dances with an invisible partner between the three couples, ending his dance at the canvas, facing away from us, as the lights fade.)

PROPS

(Props for all scenes are preset at top of show.)

LIBBY
Onstage:
Can opener
Matches
2 Ashtrays
Cocktail napkins
Cig. holder w/cigs.
Conf. sugar
2 Cans pineapple juice
Grenadine
Triple sec
Vodka
Punch bowl/ladel
5 Punch glasses
1 Rocks glass
Flower vase
2 Large pillows
1 Small pillow
2 Beer bottles

Offstage:
Cigarettes
Matches
Ashtray
White rum
Push button desk phone
Tall glass
Mussels/paper bag
Bowl for mussels
Crackers & dip tray
Cracker tray
Tooth block

Caviar
Keys
Mirror
Hammer
Tic tacs (broken tooth)
2 Cookbooks
Alarm clock
Apron
Place cards
Knife
Bandages
To do/to buy lists
Bowl w/peanuts

GRIEVER
Onstage:
8 Shirts
3 Ties
Shoe brush
Wall phone

Offstage:
Charioari bag
Hair brush
Hair dryer
Towel
Water spritzer

NORBERT
Onstage:
Jigsaw puzzle

Offstage:
Orange

Record album cover
Paper towel

TOM
Onstage:
Walkman
Guitar w/stand
Sheet music
Pencil
Joint
Cigarettes
Matches

Offstage:
Headsets
2 Beer bottles

EMILY
Onstage:
Gum
Portable TV

Offstage:
Hairbrush
Popcorn in bowl
Lavendar umbrella

BOO
Onstage:
Knapsack with:
    Sketch book
    Childs drawing
    Cigarettes
    Empty match book

Spritzer
Walkman
Flashdance tape
Italian phrase tape

Offstage:
Spider plant (small — dying)
Monster mask
Towl

ALICE
Offstage:
Virginia Woolf book
Pencils (2)
Cracker
Flowers in florist paper
2 Rubber bands
Cigarettes
Cig. lighter

COSTUME PLOT

LIBBY
Sunglasses
Beige trenchcoat w/belt
Black chiffon scarf (long)
Plastic rain bonnet
Athletic sneakers
Black slip
Black stockings
Black leather clutch purse
Blue and peach floral silk kimona.
'Zabars' apron
Black silk dress—elegant, simple, expensive
Black heels—"silk faille"
Jewelry—expensive

GRIEVER
Blue silk bathrobe—antique
"Designer" underwear
Grey/black silk pants—(pleated)
Magenta "designer" shirt—(expensive)
Hand-painted silk tie
Silk sox
Leather belt
Leather loafers—(Italian, expensive)

BOO
Grey sweatshirt (cut-off)
Blue striped tank top
Blue athletic shorts
"Stirrup" tights—purple
Headband
Beige pleated linen pants
Hand-painted geometric top (off-the-shoulder)
Ankle-sox (geometric pattern)

Heels — blue leather
"Bag of Rags" scarves

ALICE
Burgundy & blue print skirt
Beige linen overblouse
Eyeglasses — oversize, "tortoise-shell"
Periwinkle-blue silk blouse
Dove-grey leather flats
Rust suede belt
Large burgundy leather bag
Tasteful jewelry
Stockings

EMILY
Ivory China — silk blouse
Blue suede belt
Pale blue antique skirt
Grey-green wool crepe antique jacket
Handpainted patterned tights
Lavender anklets
Raw coral necklace
Brown leather antique boots (ankle high)
Chinese silk floral antique scarf

(Scene 3)
Cream colored man's shirt

TOM
Off-white shawl collared dinner jacket (antique)
Brown-on-brown print antique shirt
Taupe pleated vintage pants
Brown suspenders
Argyle sox —

Sneakers
Burnt orange antique tie

NORBERT
Blue and white athletic T-shirt (sleeveless)
Taupe sweatpants
Beige cotton pleated pants
"Designer" knitted shirt (casual)
Brown linen shoes
Sox
Handkerchief

Other Publications for Your Interest

OTHER PEOPLE'S MONEY
(LITTLE THEATRE—DRAMA)

By JERRY STERNER

3 men, 2 women—One Set

Wall Street takeover artist Lawrence Garfinkle's intrepid computer is going "tilt" over the undervalued stock of New England Wire & Cable. He goes after the vulnerable company, buying up its stock to try and take over the company at the annual meeting. If the stockholders back Garfinkle, they will make a bundle—but what of the 1200 employees? What of the local community? Too bad, says Garfinkle, who would then liquidate the company—take the money and run. Set against the charmingly rapacious financier are Jorgenson, who has run the company since the Year One and his chief operations officer, Coles, who understands, unlike the genial Jorgenson, what a threat Garfinkle poses to the firm. They bring in Kate, a bright young woman lawyer, who specializes in fending off takeovers—and who is the daughter of Jorgenson's administrative assistant, Bea. Kate must not only contend with Garfinkle—she must also move Jorgenson into taking decisive action. Should they use "greenmail"? Try to find a "White Knight"? Employ a "shark repellent"? This compelling drama about Main Street vs. Wall Street is as topical and fresh as today's headlines, giving its audience an inside look at what's *really going on* in this country and asking trenchant questions, not the least of which is whether a corporate raider is really the creature from the Black Lagoon of capitalism or the Ultimate Realist come to save business from itself.

(#17064)

THE DOWNSIDE
(LITTLE THEATRE—COMEDY)

By RICHARD DRESSER

6 men, 2 women—Combination Interior

These days, American business is a prime target for satire, and no recent play has cut as deep, with more hilarious results, than this superb new comedy from the Long Wharf Theatre. Mark & Maxwell, a New Jersey pharmaceuticals firm, has acquired U.S. rights to market an anti-stress drug manufactured in Europe, pending F.D.A. approval; but the marketing executives have got to come up with a snazzy ad campaign by January—and here we are in December! The irony is that nowhere in this drug more needed than right there at Mark & Maxwell, a textbook example of corporate ineptitude, where it seems all you have to do to get ahead is look good in a suit. The marketing strategy meetings get more and more pointless and frenetic as the deadline approaches. These meetings are "chaired" by Dave, the boss, who is never actually there—he is a voice coming out of a box, as Dave phones in while jetting to one meeting or another, eventually directing the ad campaign on his mobile phone while his plane is being hijacked! Doesn't matter to Dave, though—what matters is the possible "downside" of this new drug: hallucinations. "Ridiculous", says the senior marketing executive Alan: who then proceeds to tell how Richard Nixon comes to his house in the middle of the night to visit..."Richard Dresser's deft satirical sword pinks the corporate image repeatedly, leaving the audience amused but thoughtful."—Meriden Record. "Funny and ruthlessly cynical."—Phila. Inquirer. "A new comedy that is sheer delight."—Westport News. "The Long Wharf audience laughed a lot, particularly those with office training. But they were also given something to ponder about the way we get things done in America these days, or rather pretend to get things done. No wonder the Japanese are winning."—L.A. Times.

(#6718)

Other Publications for Your Interest

ALONE AT THE BEACH
(LITTLE THEATRE—COMEDY)
By RICHARD DRESSER

4 men, 3 women—Combination Interior/Exterior

"So you thought the kind of comedy that sends audiences home happy had disappeared from the American theatre scene? *"Wrong!"* enthused the Louisville Courier-Journal over this literate, witty comedy, which had the audience at Actors Theatre of Louisville's famed Humana Festival whooping with laughter. George, a mild-mannered man in his mid-30's, has inherited a beach house in the Hamptons on Long Island. In order to afford to keep it, he has let out rooms to boarders, Manhattan-ites desparate to get out of the city on weekends. Blindly, and blithely, George has not actually *met* any of these denizens of the yuppie sector of the urban jungle. If everyone were Great Fun and Easy To Get Along With, everyone would have a great time—but the audience, of course, wouldn't. Who wants to watch a bunch of friendly, well-adjusted people have Fun In The Sun? Thankfully, Dresser gives us a motley crew of urban neurotics, male and female, who begin to drive George, and everyone else, crazy the moment they arrive. Somehow, though, everyone survives the experience, egos intact; and, in fact, some of the most unlikely romances develop, before everyone has to face reality: Labor Day and, subsequently, the trek back to New York City for good—until next summer? "Has a unique sparkle." New Albany Tribune. "A winner...a riotously funny sex farce."—Detroit News. "A charming romp that should turn up in regional and community theatres all over the place."—Houston Post. "Has the pacing of a Neil Simon script but with some of the dry, more cerebral wit of Jules Feiffer."—Evansville Courier.

(#3118)

EMILY
(ADVANCED GROUPS—SERIOUS COMEDY)
By STEPHEN METCALFE

8 men, 4 women, to play a variety of roles.
Bare stage, w/drops, wings, projections & wagons; or, may be unit set.

This brilliant, cynical, contemporary new comedy by the author of *Strange Snow, Vikings, Sorrows and Sons* and *The Incredibly Famous Willy Rivers* dares to take what amounts to a politically "incorrect" stance about the successful "New Woman." Emily is a successful New York City stockbroker who mixes it up with the boys and always comes out on top. In fact, she was described by one misguided critic as coming off like a "man in drag"; because, as we all know, women are caring, loving, nurturing creatures—and what a wonderful world it would be if *they* were in positions of political and/or business power, instead of those insensitive jerks, the *men*. Emily is just as cynical and ruthless as any man in her position; until, that is, she meets a caring, sensitive, aspiring actor (in other words, a nice guy with no money) who doesn't fall for her manipulative ruses; but, rather, for the real Emily he sees inside the ruthless yuppie—who may, or may not, exist. "Glorious...a sparkling comedy with bite to it. The title character is a gold mine of a role for an actress."—San Diego Tribune. "A real winner...a bravura balancing act right on the edge of sentimentality, finally and triumphantly crystalline in its emotional honesty...A triumph."—San Diego Union.

(#7076)